DIRECT DAY GAME METHOD

PICK UP GIRLS ON THE STREET, AT THE MALL OR COFFEE SHOP

CHARLIE VALENTINO

Direct Day Game Method

By Charlie Valentino

First Printing, 2012

ISBN-13: 9798640696943

CONTENTS

INTRODUCTION

Thank you for picking up your copy of Direct Day Game Method by me, Charlie Valentino.

Let's start with a question. Why do I practice direct day game and only direct day game?

The answer is simple.

In fact, that is the answer; it is the simplest method of pick up there is.

Like nearly everybody new to pick up, I once suffered from extreme approach anxiety. This was partly because I was following other people's methods and those methods were not right for me. These methods were most often complex and involved long threads, routines or stories that I found impossible to remember, never mind actually carry out, when I was under the extreme pressure of a realtime pick up situation. In order to make success easier for me, I needed a method that stripped pick up down to its bare bones and that was simple enough to implement under the kind of extreme pressure that speaking to a beautiful stranger can so often bring.

Of course, there are many ways of going about meeting women out in the real world and each situation might call for a different approach or style to get the best results. It's also true that direct day game (DDG) might not even be the one method that is best for you, however, I can only speak from my own experiences that attest to DDG consistently being the superior method for meeting women in the largest range of situations and with the highest probability of success. It is direct day game that I teach in this book.

It's my intention that after you've finished reading, you'll be familiar with my method for meeting women during the day and in a large array of situations, be it walking down the street, sitting in the coffee shop or browsing clothes at the shopping mall.

If you've read other books on the subject of meeting women then you will most likely find that some of my core beliefs will be at odds with much of what you've already learned in other places. This is because both direct and indirect, as well as day and night game have both their adherents and critics. Since it is I who has your attention this moment, all I can ask is that you read the following material with an open mind and most importantly, with a determination to implement what you learn, so you can see, and indeed live, for yourself the power that DDG bestows.

I strongly believe that DDG is the only method that novices, all novices, to the art of meeting women should use.

Having said that, DDG was just as advantageous when I was a twenty-year-old novice as it was ten years later, when I wrote the first edition of this book, as it is today while I write this second edition, given that the interim has bestowed upon me an increase in confidence, stature, wealth and status.

That's right, it's direct day game that I still use and always will.

The truth is, and this goes for any field, that whether novice or advanced, the simplest methods are usually the best. Due to the anxiety that is so often involved, this is especially true when meeting women.

DDG does not weigh the man down with techniques, tactics, routines, games, stories or anything else. DDG works so perfectly because it's just you and her in the moment with no mind-debilitating crap flying around inside your head. This is the surest way of reducing, or even eliminating, the crippling anxiety that so often prevents men from making an approach at all.

Although the years since writing the first edition have helped to refine my technique, I intend to also keep this second edition as short as possible. There already exists many books that cover approaching and dating women from every conceivable angle, some of which teach skills that should be considered advanced. Might I ask what good any of this information is whilst in the heat of your early approaches? How much of it will you even remember? How much of it will you be able to act upon?

One of my core principles is to keep the approach stripped down as much as possible and to discard anything that's not absolutely essential. It's this streamlined approach that all but guarantees a clear head when it's most needed.

With the intro out of the way, let's now begin the journey of discovering the simplest and most effective strategy that exists for meeting women.

DAY GAME VERSUS NIGHT GAME

There are many reasons why I prefer approaching women during the day over approaching at night in bars, pubs or night clubs, and you can believe me when I say that there are two very different dynamics dependent on *when* you choose to approach, two very different mindsets from both your own perspective and hers.

First, and most important of all, the night is when she is at her most powerful and you are at your least, so unless you're in the top 10% of men when it comes to physical attractiveness then this puts you at a severe disadvantage. Every guy in the club is already looking at her and you're just another one of those guys, no matter how good your game might be. For me, it's just too much competition and effort for potentially too little return. Let me explain...

At night, even if you do manage to out-game the hundred

other guys all aiming to take her home, that's all it's ever likely to be, a one night stand, which of course is fine if that's what you're going for but realistically, unless you're one of those men who waits around to catch a drunken harlot stumbling out after closing time, and thus opening yourself up to a sexual assault allegation, then how many nights on the town will you need to endure before you finally hook up with someone, anyone, let alone a girl you're actually attracted to. Again, irrespective of the very real risks now involved in the #MeToo era, unless you're an exceptionally attractive guy, then it's a lot of effort for very little return and speaking for myself, as a man of high-value, I'd much rather stay home, save my money, and read a fitness or investment book than have a guaranteed lay with a woman I'm just barely excited by. And as for attempting to have something "more" by instead asking for her number, well, numbers scored at the club are amongst the flakiest of them all and that's *if* she even remembers ever giving it to you.

If you enjoy bars and clubs then, by all means, go and have fun, but do so to spend time with your friends rather than to meet women because honestly, there are far better and more time-efficient ways of getting exactly what you want.

By switching to DDG, you immediately eliminate all competition. With DDG you will stand out and will be remembered, and even if your approach does not go as well as hoped, you'll still be respected because you'll be the only guy that week, month, year or perhaps even in her entire life who actually had the balls to approach whilst she was walking along Main Street carrying her shopping.

FAKE

Women dress up when they go out at night, they apply makeup, wear padded bras, push out their breasts and put on a facade that even those closest to her would not recognise. Guys do this too, of course. We push out our chests, suck in our guts, act macho when normally we wouldn't, and just being around so many women revealing flesh, thus causing arousal, serves to shave ten points off our IQs. That's not a joke. Men lose intelligence when they're aroused. Nature has had to learn to trick men into making babies, which makes sense when thinking about it logically because, even though we might well love them, children are an extreme burden and there can be little denying they compromise our own ambitions and happiness. By making us dumber around women, we're more likely to procreate. Add alcohol and competition induced male bravado and, well, it's something I could do without.

All this taken together means that at night, we're not getting the real girl just as she's not getting the real man. Of course, this might be one of those scenarios where you might just think to yourself "who cares," and if you only want to get laid then I'd be inclined to agree with that sentiment. However, if you're interested in something more, then this is just one additional reason why day game wins out.

In the shopping mall, you get the real person. Therefore, if she turns out to be a bitch, then you can be sure it's real and that you'd be better off without her.

SHIT TESTING

Let's be honest here. Most men only have the balls to approach women during the night, and even then, it's only after they've tanked up heavily on shots. What does this say about him? If he wasn't drunk, would he even have the balls to be making an approach? The answer is probably not. Of course, women know this instinctively and over time, they hone this instinct to perfection in order to weed out these low-value cowards who need alcohol before daring to initiate a conversation. This is why they use what has become known as the "shit test."

Women use shit tests all the time. They do it to test a man's worth, his value, his purpose, and most importantly of all, to find out where he is in the hierarchy in comparison to herself. Because women only date up (a phenomenon in nature known as hypergamy), if you fail the shit test then she will logically conclude that you are beneath her and thus, you will be discarded.

By approaching a woman at night, you will almost certainly be confronted with a shit test immediately, usually at around the point you say "hi," and she rolls her eyes and turns her back to you. If you manage to get past this (by persisting and showing how unruffled you are) then the next test will likely come when she gestures to her empty glass and implies that you should buy her a drink, and rounds for all her friends too.

By now, most guys in this situation, perhaps 95% of them, will either walk away indignantly and tell their mates that she was a bitch or worse, he will buy them all drinks. Either way, he's failed the test. Perhaps only 5% of men are able to think on their feet and use secret option number three, which involves remaining unruffled whilst not caving in to her demands and coming up with something funny, witty or disarming, a middle path, so to speak. You have about a second to figure out what that middle path might be, to decide what to say, and you must do this whilst under the gaze of the hot girl you want to take home, as well as all her friends. If you do manage to come up with something, perhaps a witty retort that has her in stitches, then congratulations, all you have to do now is prepare for her next shit test that's sure to come soon.

Assuming you then pass this next test, as well as all the others, by this point, what kind of man even wants anything to do with her.

It's only because women in clubs and bars get hit on all the time, and mostly by men who they perceive to be of lower value, that they feel the need to put on this 'act.' And because it's the hotter girls who get hit on more often, you will not be surprised to learn that it's these same girls who're more likely to use shit tests and the more shit tests they're likely to use.

Shit tests are a self-defence mechanism, to save her time, if nothing else. If she engaged with every single guy who came up to speak with her, not only would she be left with no time to engage with men she was actually interested in but she'd have little time to speak with her friends either. Worst of all, she'd be perceived as a slut and the slut is always the girl in town with the lowest sexual market value. This is bad reproductive strategy on her part.

You can avoid the severity and frequency of shit tests by either restricting your approaches to the lowest and most unattractive of women, or by working on yourself until you become one of the top 10% of men but even then, she will still do it, but that doesn't mean to say that you, as a man of high-value, needs to place yourself in a position where you have to deal with it. Not when there are alternatives.

No, during the day you get the real girl and not some act or persona she's putting on whilst she's out with her friends.

BALLS

However, those few guys, perhaps a percentage as low as 0.01% who actually have the balls to approach women in the street, in broad daylight without the effects of alcohol running through their systems will not have to endure any such crap as the shit test. This is overwhelmingly because by making the approach in the first place, as long as the approach is handled tactfully, then you've already demonstrated superior value, hence there is little need to shit test. During the day you get the real person, the real girl and you can just skip the facade, all the fake bullshit and just get straight to the point. That point is this: You saw her, you like her and you want her contact information.

Did I tell you that day game was simple?

MOTHER HENS

At night, you also have to contend with her group of friends.

Sure, if you've read other pick up manuals, you'll know all about using your own friends to take care of hers whilst you speak to the girl you're interested in. But are your friends willing to be your bag boy? How good at speaking to women are your friends? Are they capable of distracting them long enough for you to get to know your girl? Or will her friends get annoyed or jealous and pull her away?

That's a lot of shit you have absolutely no control over and let's face it, the only women who go to bars without their friends are prostitutes. This means that at night, you *will* have to contend with mother hens.

However, during the day, women are most often out by themselves so there's no need to worry about any of this. And if you do see a girl you'd like to approach who's not alone, remember that daytime dynamics are very different. There's no cock blocking in the street or at Starbucks, at least not to the same extent, and besides, if your direct approach is done right, if you also acknowledge the hen, then at the very least, any other women present will be too impressed to be anything but totally polite towards you.

RELATIONSHIP

I won't linger much on the point that you're also far more likely to meet quality women during the day because it's obvious. In bars, it's a mixed bag of women at best but during the day, it's so easy locating women who share your interests, whether it be skiing, lifting, tennis or gaming, merely by putting yourself in front of those people, by hanging out where these people hang out. You are far more likely to meet a better quality of person, definitely the relationship kind of a girl, in a coffee shop over a bar, the library over a night club. Women much prefer telling their family they met a guy at yoga class than in a bar. It just sounds so much nicer.

If it's a relationship you're hoping to find then you definitely want to be meeting women during the day, in which case, this book is a perfect fit for you.

DIRECT VERSUS INDIRECT

For the longest time, it was the indirect method that was preferred amongst most of the acclaimed and experienced dating coaches and gurus, however, I think that by now, most of the old schoolers have come around to the direct method of approaching women, at least with regards the daytime. I've also started noticing that most newcomers now appear to prefer the direct method too and I suspect the reason for this is that they're having better results over the alternative, now that more people are attempting it in place of the indirect approach. This appears to be universal, in that what's true in Europe, happens to be true in the Americas, happens to be true in Asia. What works here, works there. Human nature is human nature.

If you're unsure exactly what the indirect method of approach entails, I shall clarify now.

Indirect is where you approach a girl under the radar

with some pretext for initiating a conversation. You might start by asking a question, for the time, directions or for her opinion on something. For example, in Starbucks you might ask a girl what she thinks is the better drink, mocha or latte, because you're new to coffee shops and don't have much of an idea what is what. At this point, everything appears normal and usual. She would then answer your question. Typically, your next move would be to elaborate on her response in order to extend the interaction beyond her answer, maybe by delving into the finer aspects of lattes and why she thinks you should order one over a mocha. The two of you would talk about lattes for a couple of minutes, exciting stuff, whilst you're using the time to find something special or unique to her that stands out, something to compliment her on. Perhaps she's wearing a distinctive piece of clothing, jewellery or maybe you're interested in the book she's reading (you're pretending to be, at least). The aim is to take the conversation away from lattes and onto something more personal so you can move the pick up attempt onto the next stage. After complimenting the bracelet or book, you might try to find a connection, maybe that your sister has a similar bracelet or you heard it was a good book. Ok, cool. Here would be a suitable time to introduce yourselves and shake hands. The next is the most crucial part of the entire indirect attempt because you're suddenly shifting into a different mode. You are no longer talking about lattes and are now attempting instead to become acquainted. From this point forward, she might be expected to slip the word "boyfriend" into the conversation in order to subtly let you know she has one, or that she's not interested. So, how much time have you wasted up until this point? Five or ten minutes perhaps to find out she has a boyfriend. But let's assume she's single and the pick up continues. You now have to subtly qualify yourself to demonstrate that you're worth her attention and to gain attraction, thus winning her over. You have to do this because you didn't go direct, which in itself is all the qualification you need to prove your worth. Typically, you might qualify yourself by telling a few stories, perhaps about a cool adventure you've recently taken, or a qualification you have. The intention behind this is to impress her, though without being too obvious about it, which is why you need to remember a few stories that will do the work for you. If you recently came back from a trip around the world or sold your movie script then maybe she'll be impressed. Now let's assume she's opening up, getting involved in the interaction and is also telling you something about herself. The next aim is to attempt to get her to qualify herself to you, to invest in you. You might do this by asking her questions like, "tell me three things about yourself that will impress me." When she gives her answer, you need to act impressed, the approach is going well. Next, you have to discover some common ground, a reason to see each other again, just the two of you in a more social setting. Hopefully, you will already have gaged this common ground information, or perhaps she already imparted her interests with the earlier qualification question. If you both like the movies or going hiking, for example, then you have a logical date right there and from then, it's only a matter of asking for her number.

The long paragraph above is a very basic model for an indirect pick up. Of course, there are countless additional tactics that may also be used, especially if you're inclined to make your life more complicated than it needs to be, such as kino escalation (always a good idea), routines, jokes, games, NLP, cold reads, push/pull etc. But I'm hoping you're beginning to see just why I wanted an easier method of approaching women.

I won't lie and say the indirect method does not have its place. It does indeed work for a great many people and when you look at the structure from a practical standpoint, it's fundamentally just a normal interaction between two human beings, with a few subtle psychology tricks thrown in for attraction purposes.

On the flip side, there are indeed situations where I would recommend a more indirect approach over what I advocate for in this book. If for example you're interested in a girl inside your extended social circle, perhaps someone on your college course, then a direct approach definitely would not be recommended in that instance. Remember the immortal words DON'T SHIT WHERE YOU EAT, because if your approach falls through then you'll forever be known as *that socially uncalibrated guy* who tried to pick up one of his college mates, which is the last thing you need if it's day one of five years. Learn from my mistakes. Yes, unfortunately, I've made this error of judgement more than once, believing too strongly in my method and that it was perfect for all daytime scenarios when in fact, it turned out not to be true. I then had to see the same girl nearly every time I went to the gym. Of course, there was nothing wrong with actually approaching, what I'm saying is that I used the wrong approach for *that* situation. What I should have done there was play a much longer game by making situational smalltalk over a period of weeks until the relationship naturally moved to the next level, an extended indirect approach, for lack of a better term, but as we know, that's not my style. What I learned was that you can't always take a one size fits all approach to anything, even pick up, and there are occasions when common sense is required. Better yet, don't shit where you eat.

So yes, I admit that direct is not always the ideal approach to take, however, I believe it to be infinitely superior to indirect, especially during the day, though I should also point out that the situations I mention above, the college and gym scenarios, both involved existing, and at least very loose, acquaintances. That is the key! Use the DDG method on strangers, not girls you occasionally see at the gym, not girls you sometimes see sitting at the opposite side of the same lecture theatre and certainly do not use the direct approach on your longtime crush. Thankfully, that leaves you with 99.99999% of women.

Now that I've shown a bit of balance and mentioned the problems with the direct approach, let's take a look at some of the problems with the indirect method. These problems start right at the beginning.

In too many instances, indirect approaches such as opinion openers just make no sense at all, which means there's a very real danger of coming over as being socially uncalibrated and then an all too common outcome is that you find yourself in a short conversation with an extremely perplexed girl. For example, it's just not logical to walk up to a girl sniffing perfume samples before asking what's good right now at the cinema, yet this is precisely what so much material suggests. I think that deep down, we, as logical thinking men, know this, which is why there is so much approach anxiety out there. True, some situational openers can be made relevant, for example, the what is best, latte or americano line, but only if you're in a coffee shop.

Of course, even using something totally relevant like asking what movie is good whilst you're standing in the cinema is still disingenuous, because obviously, you have ulterior motives and regardless, she's been groomed from birth to assume that every man who ever speaks to her is only after that one thing anyway. So why bother with the pretence? Are you not a man of high-value who knows what he wants, a man who sees a girl and is confident enough to be honest and straightforward about his intentions from the outset?

Indeed, by taking the indirect approach, you're concealing your true intentions as a man. You're supposedly approaching because you're interested in her romantically yet here you are talking about lattes, films or any number of things you don't actually care about. Speaking for myself, I have never been able to pull it off with a straight face, probably because I just find being false so difficult.

So why not just go direct?

The direct approach is so much more honest, simple and straightforward. The essence of the direct approach is that you see her, you march up to her and you tell her that you think she's hot.

The very fact you had the balls to walk up to her during the day and tell her you think she's gorgeous is all the qualification you'll ever need. It's for this reason you can pretty much skip the largest and most difficult chunk of the usual indirect pick up routine that's intended to impress her, remembering stories, routines and pretty much all the rest of the crap that bogs your head down and so often prevents you from approaching.

By approaching direct, you're also subtly communicating that your time is valuable, that you're busy, which is an extremely attractive quality in a man. It's a mindset you should aim to have.

Going direct enables you to find out, often within 5 seconds, if she has a boyfriend. You'll know because what usually happens is that she immediately thanks you for the compliment but follows up by saying that she's already in a relationship. Caveat: Don't necessarily believe this, it's often simply a natural gut response to being taken completely off-guard by something so unusual as a direct approach, but we'll discuss this later.

Of course, most women have, In fact, often been approached by random men during the day. They're called beggars, drunkards and charity workers, who approach absolutely everybody. This unfortunate reality can, in fact, be used to your advantage, and all you need do is ensure you don't look homeless, aren't drunk and aren't carrying around a clipboard. Easy. And when she realises you're just a normal, genuine guy who's interested in her, you'll then be able to visibly see the relief, intrigue and excitement spread across her little face.

APPROACH ANXIETY

I'll only lightly touch upon the subject of approach anxiety (AA) here because I've already written an entire book about it. If you think you suffer from AA then I will shamelessly shill for my best-selling book Destroy Approach Anxiety now. The book contains numerous strategies to make approaching women easier, spoken from my own experiences, and is an excellent accompaniment to this book. It's available on Kindle Unlimited, which means you won't pay anything if you have a subscription.

Back when I was learning my pick up theory, I found that the problem with most of the available material was that it only ever skimmed the surface of this crucial topic. Many best-selling books skipped over the subject entirely.

Even the most confident of men will often buckle at the sight of an attractive girl, a fear that often appears to compound as he learns more and more pick up material. Let me explain what I mean with a story.

Before I'd even heard about the pick up sub-culture, I actually used to have pretty good success approaching women in the street. This was despite having absolutely no idea what I was doing, I used to just blag it with my own primitive and heartfelt version of a direct approach. It wasn't until a friend introduced me to the concept of pick up and I started reading some of the available books that I actually began to fear approaching women. What I was reading overwhelmingly advocated the indirect approach. I learned about openers, transitions, kino, storytelling, closing and so much more that, taken together, really should have given me an edge. In fact, the more I learned, the more I wanted to continue learning, the intention being to become an unstoppable pick up machine.

That's when my AA began and that's when I started having less success with women.

Isn't it crazy to think that if I'd never read any books on the subject of meeting women, I'd have had greater success than I ended up having? Piecing everything together, what did I learn?

It's one of my beliefs that the fear of approaching women, be it night or day, in the street or at a bar, comes overwhelmingly from the overloading of information we learn from a variety of sources; books, internet, YouTube, etc. Men typically like to spend time studying when they gain an interest in a new field, be it fitness, investing or programming, and this should be encouraged. However, it's important to keep one concept in mind. When we discover something new, very seldom can we remember everything we've attempted to learn and usually there's a requirement to go over the same material again and again until it finally sinks in and we know it off by heart. Why is it so difficult for us to learn this way? Because repetition and regurgitation is actually how females learn. The brains of males, however, are wired differently. Our brains learn best through practical application, learning on the job, getting stuck in, just doing it, fucking up a few times and learning from our mistakes. Think about how you learn best and I'm sure you'll be able to relate. Yes, classrooms are set up to benefit females at the expense of males, but what can we do about it? But I'm sure you can see the problem when it comes to pick up. Reading books can only do so much. Yet men, because we have not been informed, will continue studying from books and videos ad infinitum regardless, perhaps in the hope that eventually they'll discover that one pick up line, that one technique or that one magic bullet that will finally make things easy.

It's this learning of so much material that's a major contributor to AA. The truth is that when it comes to indirect pick up, it actually does help to be familiar with a wide range of theory. Unfortunately, this only serves to increase AA, especially when you're starting out. How are you supposed to actually use any of these tips, tricks or techniques during your first few approaches whilst you're nervous as hell and feeling under pressure? I wouldn't say it's impossible, but you're definitely making things hard for yourself.

This is why I focus on keeping things simple.

The reason DDG works so well is primarily because you skip all the theory, you forget everything you've ever learned and instead, the approach is condensed down to its skeleton. This reduces the level of crap flying around in your head and eliminates the need to remember your next line, trick or tactic. It instead brings you into the moment, just you and her having a conversation as real people.

This is another reason why I only advocate for DDG, especially for men who are just getting started. When you're starting, you really need the simplest method there is, the strategy that will first enable you to get as many successful approaches as you need under your belt before you even think about supplementing your style with any fancy additional techniques you read about on some forum. My advice is only to experiment with unnecessary extras after you've defeated any AA you might have, even though by using the good standard DDG approach I teach here, there will be little need for any of it anyway.

AA never completely goes away. You might even one day find yourself returning to pick up after a long relationship and feel like you're back to where you started, which is when you'll return to DDG and be thankful that NLP is not a requirement for getting a girl's number.

What good are push/pull routines, NLP and magic tricks anyway if you've never even approached a woman cold in the street? How can any normal guy be expected to pull off that kind of shit on their first few approaches whilst their knees are shaking and their head is spinning? Your brain will scramble, you will forget what you think you know and even if you don't, you will not feel comfortable doing it anyway.

DDG takes this into account.

DDG is different because there are so very few elements to it, which means that when you're in an interaction with a hot girl and the people in your periphery become blurs as they pass you by, there's very little that can cause your brain to seize up.

You might think this is a short book, and indeed it is, but I hope now you realise that that's the whole point. Believe me, I'm doing you a favour by keeping it short. So enough of the rambling, let's finally delve into the dynamics of direct day game.

PRE-APPROACH

Whether you're going out especially to talk to women or you're merely going about your daily business, it always pays to be prepared, just on the off-chance you see someone you like.

Always take these pre-approach measures and the next time action is called for, you'll be able to jump straight into seduction mode.

ALWAYS LOOK YOUR BEST

Many of the excuses we create to make ourselves feel better about not approaching come from going out not looking our best.

It's so easy not to approach a hot girl because we know we didn't leave the house in our best clothes or a decent pair of shoes or because we decided not to shave that day.

We must remove these excuses.

If we leave the house every day knowing we look awesome then we're eliminating one of the main reasons for not approaching.

But more importantly than that, if we look our best then we'll feel ten times more confident when making an approach. You really do need to leave the house every day feeling unstoppable, and looking and feeling great is such a huge part of this.

There's not really much else to say about it other than; good grooming and dress well.

Another thing you should be doing as a more long term goal is to build a good physique. While women are not as interested in looks as we men are, I'd be lying if I said looks weren't important. A strong body on a man is an attractive feature to a woman but more importantly than that, if you have a great body then you'll feel ten times more confident than if you were overweight. Having been overweight myself, I can attest to the difference you feel after losing it.

If you are overweight then take up weight lifting and high-intensity interval training which, along with an improved diet, will have a marked effect on how you look, feel and perceive yourself.

BE SPONTANEOUS

When you're out and about, I've found it's far easier to approach if you don't make picking up girls your reason for being out in the first place.

It's funny, but not only do they hardly ever seem to appear when you're actively searching, but doing so is to walk about in a constant state of nervousness. All this means is that if you do find a cute girl then you'll already be in a state of sweats and what often happens is that your voice quivers too. Talk about creating unnecessary anxiety for yourself.

DDG is supposed to be real. When you walk around town looking for targets it ceases to be real, it ceases to be genuine and it's just one of those things that women are very good at picking up on.

It's far better to always look your best and have no intention of actually making any approaches so that if you do see a nice lady then you'll be able to snap straight into approach mode, and when you worship the zero second rule, you can arrive in a genuine state of excitement.

This tip does indeed take my approach style into account. DDG is supposed to be genuine, which means spontaneous. You need to be as surprised as she will be when you find yourself suddenly talking to a hot girl when ten seconds earlier, you were innocently on your way to the gym.

The rule is this: You see her, you're already walking towards her.

LISTEN TO UPBEAT MUSIC

This one is optional, but is also a top tip I've included in Destroy Approach Anxiety because listening to motivational songs can really put you in the mood for approaching. They can also make you feel and sound upbeat when you arrive.

The best songs would be those that have personal relevance to yourself. Songs that hype me up won't necessarily be the same songs that work for you. Having said that, I once researched popular, universal motivational songs and did long ago have quite a large list. Unfortunately, my hard drive got wiped and I lost a lot of them. However, there are some classics that have always remained in my head, which goes to show how memorable they are and you too should have them on standby.

Listen to the music as you're approaching and remove

your earplugs just before speaking. That's how to make it spontaneous.

Here's my list but remember to add your own:

Greatest Day – Take That

Believe – Josh Groban

Eye of the Tiger – Survivor

Gotta Be Somebody – Nickelback

I Believe I Can Fly – R. Kelly

It's A Beautiful Life – Ace of Base

It's My Life – Bon Jovi

March On – Good Charlotte (highly recommended)

You Gotta Be – Des'ree

Hero – Mariah Carey

Beautiful Day – U2

Nessun Dorma – Pavarotti

Affirmation – Savage Garden

Song 2 – Blur

Beautiful One – Suede

I Won't Back Down – Tom Petty

I Feel Good – James Brown

Tub Thumping – Chumba Wumba (another great choice)

One Day More – Les Miserables

My Way – Frank Sinatra

Everybody's Free (To Wear Sunscreen) – Baz Luhrmann

Go Your Own Way – Fleetwood Mac / Lissie from the Twinings Ad

CONFIDENCE - THE MOST IMPORTANT INGREDIENT

Surveys of women repeatedly reveal that the most attractive trait they look for in a man is confidence. Confidence beats height, money and looks.

What kind of men approach women cold and direct in the street? The answer is obviously confident men. When you approach women in a direct way, they'll naturally assume you to be confident, therefore, it's important to live up to this expectation and not to let them down.

If you're new to this then unfortunately, and I'm going to be honest with you here, it will take a few approaches and even a few setbacks before you do become confident at approaching. But don't let this put you off because the thing about making even a bad approach is that as soon as it's over, you will immediately feel the change in your mood and that change will be to one of confidence. It's incredible how confident you feel after making the day's first approach, even a bad one, and in the early stages, you will feel a huge burden lift from your shoulders, "I made a fucking approach, I'm not dead, I actually had fun, I really can fucking do this!" This has a positive spiraling effect that will endure into your next approach, therefore you should utilize this high to make even more approaches off the back of the first.

You need to appear as if you don't give a damn whether or not the approach goes amazingly well or really bad. Confident men don't care either way because a guy who's confident wouldn't let the outcome of one approach effect his state, and he certainly wouldn't allow a potentially negative opinion of a female to effect him either.

For those who think looking and sounding confident will be an issue, you'll be pleased to know that faking confidence is easy. Here are some useful tips to follow:

- First and foremost, as already mentioned, confident men dress well, they're well-groomed and this in turn bestows upon them even more confidence. When you're well-dressed, have you ever noticed how you stand with your head held just that little bit higher. Have you ever noticed how you walk with a spring in your step? This leads to our next point.
- You need to ensure your walk is upright and with an excellent posture. This in itself will give you power which you'll feel running through your body. You need to walk with your chin up,

shoulders pulled back, chest out a little bit, pull your tummy in and walk with a deliberate purpose. If you struggle with this then just imagine there's a helium balloon attached to your chin and it's pulling your entire head upwards. That always seems to do the trick.

- Make no apologies for approaching your target and interrupting her day. You're a man, you've seen somebody attractive that you'd like to talk to and it's she who should be thankful for it.

- Whilst conversing, it's vitally important to speak in a slow and controlled manner. Confident people speak slowly because they don't expect anybody will interrupt them. Try it when you next speak to your friends. Experiment speaking fast and speaking slowly. See which makes you sound more in control of the situation. Speaking slowly will make you sound much more authoritative. It will also serve to allay your nerves (for reasons I'll talk about more in the approach section), which will in turn prevent the girl from becoming nervous in your presence.

- When you speak, alternate the pitch of your voice. Few people speak with varying pitches and it's an interesting and even attractive trait to have. Listen to how news readers, game show hosts and movie stars speak and try and learn from them. This will make you appear captivating, not to mention confident.

- It's important to use body language when speaking. Body language shows you're in control of the situation and are not afraid to take up a little bit of space. Simply bend your arms at the elbows and make small gestures as you speak. You can make slightly larger gestures to emphasize a point. Practice in the mirror. Be careful not to overdo it though or it can look staged.
- When you're standing, widen your stance and take up a little extra space. This shows dominance and makes you appear more 'rooted.'
- Your movements need to be slow and controlled. Again, only confident people make slow movements, like nothing in the world bothers them. Just think how fast and erratic movements make people seem nervous. Make sure you do the opposite.
- A simple thing for you not to do is to cross or fold your arms. This makes you appear defensive and uncomfortable. Remember to keep your arms bent at the elbow, perhaps even clasp your hands together in front.
- An obvious tip is not to fidget. Many people fidget without even realising and it always blows your cover as a confident man. Keep your hands away from your face and resist the urge to play with your phone.
- Confident men make eye contact! This is obvious.

The crazy thing is, and studies have proven this, that if you project these confident mannerisms, not only do you look confident in the eyes of other people, but you actually start to feel the confidence within yourself. It's a case of life imitating art.

An easy way of explaining this in a more practical sense is that when you have your arms crossed, you actually feel more closed off. However, when you unfold your arms, you naturally open up.

Body language is powerful! Please don't underestimate this section.

If you're ever in an interaction with a girl and she's not enjoying herself, she's very likely to fold her arms. When this next happens, try making a funny statement and then give her a high five. Maybe you can introduce yourself and shake her hand. If after either of these she hasn't re-folded her arms, you will notice how she begins to open up and become more friendly and talkative. If she now feels more relaxed, she'll be less likely to again fold her arms.

If before approaching, you've done everything listed above, then if she happens to see you walking up to her, she should be fairly warm and receptive when you arrive and start talking. Remember that during the day, women rarely get approached by well-groomed men with good intentions. If you've done all the above right then she will be thrilled to meet you.

THE APPROACH

Now we're getting to the fun part and the reason you bought this book.

The DDG approach will work just about anywhere during the day, the main places being; the street, coffee shop, shopping mall and college or university campuses. All you have to do is tailor the DDG approach to your current venue as necessary but trust me, save for the occasional shift in positions, there's really not much difference between approaching in the coffee shop and approaching in the library or street.

The information you're about to learn may sound so simple that you'll find it hard to believe it works so well. Trust me, this method works so well *because* it's simple. Please keep an open mind and read the following pages with a determination to try what you learn. The thought of being one of the few men who can walk up to any girl he pleases knowing he has an excellent chance of getting her number, a date or more is incredibly empowering.

We shall now cover every element of the direct daytime approach, step by step.

WALKING TOWARDS HER

The majority of the time, you'll see your target either standing or walking in the street. You must approach immediately. The only excuse you have for not approaching immediately is if you haven't yet decided if you find her attractive. Get a better view or go regardless. If she turns out to have a face like a plasterer's radio then you can abort before announcing your presence.

Sometimes the street will be busy, other times it will be quiet, sometimes she will be alone, other times she will have company. If it's busy then you might wish to follow her so you can time your move for a suitable opening where there are fewer people, if this is something you're overly bothered about. Remember, she might prefer more discretion herself but in general, I've found that women don't care much about how many other people are in the vicinity and some women even love the extra attention. This is your preference, though the more you do this, the less you'll care about who else might be around.

At this stage, the aim is to get <u>in front</u> of her, which very often means you have to alter the angle of approach so that she can see you coming.

Never approach from behind, it hardly ever achieves good results. No tapping her on the shoulder from her blind spot either. I repeat, you must get in front so she can see you approaching. If she's walking away then this might involve having to walk past her before angling around in an arc so that you can appear in front. This is important. Sometimes she will see you walking in a strange semi-circle before doubling back on yourself to approach her. This is all part of the fun and it's never been a problem.

Sometimes, you will have to run to get in front of her, especially if she's walking with a purpose. Don't worry, the direct approach is all about impact and the need to run, or walk fast, only adds to the impact and makes everything appear more spontaneous and real. I've had to do this in flip-flops, which isn't easy, but it did not detract from my approach. Keep in mind, however, that the faster she is walking, the more space you will have to leave her when you step out in her path.

When you stop in front of her, and I repeat, in front, not from the side and definitely not from behind, you need to give her around two whole metres of space. To put this in perspective, it should be the length of you lying down on the floor and then another half of you added on top. The reason for this is twofold. Firstly, it'll make her feel more comfortable. Homeless guys, charity muggers, real muggers and beggars will not give her room, which is why you must telegraph that you're different. The second reason is that the girl will not be expecting to be approached, which means she'll almost certainly continue walking for at least a couple paces before her brain even realises there's somebody standing in her trajectory.

When I say trajectory, what I mean is you're not standing "directly" in her path. You don't want her to crash into you. The angle you're allowing is around thirty degrees or five past the hour. What this does is remove the potential of coming across as a threat, whilst still being imposing enough to show your confidence and worth, a sensible middle ground that still ensures she stops.

Shopping malls can be easy. Often she'll be stood still, window shopping or at the most, walking slow under the weight of her bags. If she's not moving then you can give a little bit less space but use your judgement.

Seated girls are easiest because, obviously, the target's not moving, which means you can also get a good look before strolling up. She also has time on her hands, which means she's very likely to be receptive. This goes for park benches or the coffee shop, there's no difference between the two in how you need to treat the approach.

On rare occasions you'll find my favourite approach

target of them all, girls hobbling along on crutches, so take full advantage of these gifts because she ain't going anywhere fast and might even be grateful for the respite and of course, if you find yourself in an awkward silence then there's the obvious question to ask about why she can't stand herself :)

STOPPING HER

Right, you're standing in front of her. Congratulations. Now we need to get her to stop.

But wait, Charlie, a full section on this tiny point? Yes, though you should think of stopping her as a continuation of the last section because the two so closely phase together.

You might not believe me when I say this, but the hardest part of the DDG approach is actually getting her to stop, which is why this gets a heading all of its own. Please don't overlook the importance of what I'm about to say and I suggest visualizing my instructions so you can get a clear picture of what it is in your mind. DDG might be simple, but it's not always easy.

What you need to do is make a stop gesture with both your hands.

Imagine someone is about to run straight into you. What

you would instinctively do is lock your shoulders so that your upper arms are pointing down and flex your elbows to ninety-degree angles with your fingers pointing up and palms facing out, ready to brace for impact.

This is not how we do it here.

Instead, your elbows need to be flexed at forty-five-degree angles so that your thumbs are about level with her stomach. Your fingers are pointing straight out but relaxed, like how a wizard might look doing a magic spell.

Remember, your body is at a thirty-degree angle to hers, which means you're not standing directly in her path. That's why you're instead using your hands and arms to make sure she stops because your body isn't doing the work for you. If you were to put your hands up as I described earlier, as in shielding yourself from someone running into you, then it would almost certainly intimidate her. When your hands are in this other relaxed pose, however, they're instead disarming, friendly even, and not at all threatening. Practice it.

You can augment the non-threatening stance with your feet and body positioning. When you arrived in front of her, you'll naturally have had one foot in front of the other. Instead of standing with level feet as you normally would, keep one foot in front of the other. You can then tilt your weight back over the rear foot so that you're leaning very slightly back. Bring your hands up into the relaxed stop gesture at the same time your body tilts back, trying to make it look smooth. This looks so much cooler and will further make her feel comfortable.

You say your first word to her, either "hi," or "hey," is best, as you're bringing your hands up and tilting back over your rear foot.

This is the point at which she will stop.

Does this always work? No. But years of experience tells me that this method has the best chance of getting her to stop whilst not coming across in any way as unhinged. These days, it will work for me 90% of the time. For novices, a success rate of 60% is reasonable.

Having belief helps. Not just belief in yourself but belief that she'll stop. This belief serves to give your eyes, voice and posture that little extra something that compels her to stop. She will stop if you believe it.

If you're not feeling it, if you're lacking the belief in yourself then this will manifest in your body language and you might very well come over as just another broken charity worker looking for signups or a beggar asking for money.

If she doesn't stop, don't feel bad, you've not been rejected, she just rejected your approach, not you as a person. Always analyse what went wrong because at this early stage, it's usually something that can easily be fixed and learned from. The most likely answer is that you simply did not give her enough room, which means she probably felt intimidated. That's an easy fix right there.

How was your angle? Were you too much out of her way and therefore not quite imposing enough? If she fails to stop then it's almost always likely to be for one of those two reasons.

One last thing, for your own pride, if a girl continues walking, just say nothing and carry on with your day. Don't tell her how hot you think she is to her back. What I've seen happen is that guys panic and follow through with the approach (his opener), calling it out when she's already going and isn't turning back. If she doesn't stop, she doesn't deserve your gift.

Read over these first two sections again and practice everything up to this point, until you have the movement and positioning down in one smooth motion. Try it with an imaginary moving target or a male friend. Likewise, watch a friend performing this manoeuvre and critique his performance.

THE DIRECT OPENER

You've just said your pre-opener (hey or hi) and she's stopped.

Try relating to what's going through her mind at this moment.

She has no idea what's about to happen and possibly she's even a little disorientated. With all that adrenaline pumping, you're probably feeling excitable yourself. At this point, you've both stopped, which means she's not going anywhere and if you rush into your opener then chances are that she won't fully understand what you're saying, it'll be a blur for her, so take a couple seconds of silence so she can find her feet and you can concentrate on how you're about to project your voice.

Now, the beauty of the direct opener is that you can use the same modified line over and over again in almost any situation. It only needs tailoring to suit your own style or regional dialect and so forth. It's not even anything you need to remember, unlike a typical pick up line, and even saying the words without any thought can have the positive effect of making it sound more spontaneous and dramatic.

Remember to maintain eye contact.

Here are some variations of what I usually say:

"Hey, I was just walking over there and I saw you and thought, oh my God, she is stunning, so I just had to come over and say hi."

Or...

"Hey, I was just stood over there with my friends and I saw you and thought, wow, she is stunning, so I literally just had to run away from them so I could say hi to you. I hope you're friendly too?"

Or for the coffee shop...

"Hey, I just saw you as I was queuing up for my latte and thought to myself, oh my God, she looks absolutely stunning and so I just had to come over and say hi and find out if you were friendly too? May I take a seat?"

You can see that all direct openers involve putting your heart on your sleeve and declaring your intention immediately. You'll also notice that at no point am I apologizing for "interrupting your day," (my fellow Brits, I'm talking to you). You're a man, remember, this is what real men do and there's no need to be sorry for it. Besides, you're about to make her day.

You might have noticed that two of the above examples involved asking if she's friendly too. This is a psychological trick I sometimes use, which you can add to the end of your opener if you wish, but I'll explain more about that and why I do it later on.

Now, what I'm about to say is important.

Your opener needs to be delivered slowly and calmly. There's a reason we covered speaking slowly in the confidence section and it's why I also suggest using your two-second pause to concentrate on how you're about to project your voice because I know all too well from experience that if you're not focusing on your voice, then it's going up by several octaves and when that happens there's no coming back.

Speaking too fast is almost as bad as speaking too high. We speak fast when we're nervous, though in a pick up situation this comes over as lacking faith in ourselves because we don't truly believe we're in the girl's league and therefore she won't stick around to hear us out if we're not fast about it. Either way, it's not good, so instead do the opposite. Speak slow.

Do you remember what I was saying about life imitating art? Your mind will take its cue from your body or in this case, your voice. Concentrate on sounding slightly slower than what feels natural, this will also save you from stuttering the words. If you can focus on sounding slow with a calm, deep voice, then you will come across as being confident. Nailing this will bring the added bonus of helping her to feel relaxed, often you will visibly see it in her expression, and when that happens, it bounces back on you so that you feed off each other and then you're as good as gold. It's no secret that moods can be contagious and you set the mood from the start, not with what your first words are, but by how they're perceived by her.

Your voice speed and tonality, therefore, are two things that should be given your full consideration.

THE INTRODUCTION

So after you've stated your opening line, now is the right time to introduce yourself.

Tell her what your name is and hold out your hand. It should go something like this:

"Hey, I was just walking over there and I saw you and thought, oh my God, she is stunning, so I just had to come over and say hi. I'm Brad," which is when you hold out your hand.

Remember that at this point, you're almost certainly still standing around two metres away from her, so this is your opportunity to close the gap.

Reach forward whilst saying, "I'm Brad," or whatever it is and shake her hand. She will respond with hers.

What you need to do is maintain the handshake for longer than you normally would a random person you're meeting for the first time. If she didn't get your intentions from your opener, make sure she knows it from the handshake, but obviously don't hold on too long that it becomes creepy. Use your best judgement.

Now you've done that, you'll be standing at a normal conversational distance, so position yourself at where's natural for you.

Because you've used a direct opener, it's obvious what your intention is. Therefore, if there's already another man in the picture, it's at this point the girl will usually thank you for your interest but say she has a boyfriend. Often, she will have a boyfriend but not mention it, though because there's no way you can possibly know the truth of the matter, there's no guilt on your part.

Regardless, what I can say for certain is that this response is often blurted out as an instinctual reaction to being approached. Remember the shit test from earlier? Well, it still exists during the day because women will shit test even their husbands until the day they die, but day game shit tests are far weaker than their nighttime counterparts.

When it happens, and it definitely will, my advice is not to let it change your game plan. You came so far getting to this point. My typical answer to the boyfriend response is simply to say in a nice, playful tone "you don't have a boyfriend," possibly with an additional wink and a little nudge with my elbow. What this does is show you're playful and not phased in the slightest, which serves to persuade her that maybe she was being a little hasty in her gut reaction, if it was one, or that you've defeated her shit test, if that's what it was.

If it's true and she does indeed have a boyfriend, then it's at this point she will nearly always respond in an equally playful tone, "I have." If this happens then, unfortunately, you've found one of the good ones but you can't have her. And hope that your next girlfriend does the exact same thing when someone like you next stops her in the street. At this point, you should wish her well and move on.

If, as is so often the case, she does not, in fact, have a boyfriend, then what usually happens now is she will smile and ask for you to repeat your name or ask some other question and when that happens you can smile knowing you've made the next level and can continue with the seduction.

POST OPENER - TRANSITION

After actually getting your target to stop, it's the transition that's the hardest part of the direct pick up. This is because you've finished with the only scripted part there is and now you have to actually think on your feet. Your brain has also just realised that, holy shit, you're speaking to a hot girl in a crowded street, autopilot has disengaged, and you're beginning to recognize you're on your own. At this stage, it's not uncommon to start feeling your knees shake. Even now, my knees still do this and I doubt they'll ever stop. Sometimes my foot taps involuntarily against the ground and I have to force myself not to stand arms akimbo, which betrays my nerves.

The transition involves bridging the gap between your opener and a normal conversation. Her head may still be coming to terms with what's happening so we need to do something to give her a few extra seconds in order to allow her brain time to adjust to the fact she's being hit on by a nice, friendly guy.

The transition should involve making some kind of a comment or statement that's specific to her. It should ideally not be a question though, a trap that's all too easy to fall into out of comfort. The reason you don't want to ask a question is because it's too early. How would you feel if a stranger walked up to you, said "hi," and then expected you to do all the work in keeping the conversation going, essentially placing the burden on somebody else for what they initiated. You must bear the weight of the responsibility, at least for a short while extra. That's why we don't ask a question but instead make a statement.

What was it specifically about this girl that you liked? What was it about her that caught your attention? There has to have been something. Something more than "she was just hot," because remember, you've almost certainly already said that in your opener, so you don't want to say it again because you'd be handing over all your power and putting yourself at her mercy. Women only date UP! Remember that.

Again, what specifically have you noticed about her? Is she wearing a cute scarf? Was she walking like she owns the town? Here are some suggestions:

"You know, you don't see many women with such a unique sense of style. That's why I wanted to meet you."

You can use this opportunity to brush her scarf with the backs of your fingers.

Or...

"*I mean look at you, in this cute little hat...*" maybe stroke her hat like you would a dog.

Or...

"*I think your hair's absolutely awesome.*" Give the bit hanging over her ear a gentle swipe.

Or...

"*I liked how you were leaning against that post like you don't give a fuck.*"

Or...

"*I could tell from the way you were patting that dog that you like going for coffee.*"

Come up with something that's real to her and you'll make her feel at ease, and if you can make her laugh then I won't lie, but that won't count against you either.

Of course, many women have that generic clone look to them, so if you can't think of anything to say about her specifically then you could comment about the crazy situation you've just put the both of you in.

"*You should slow down when you walk, I had to sprint to catch up with you and now I'm exhausted.*"

Or...

"You know, you made me ditch all my friends so you'd better be worth it."

Or...

"Wow, you're making me do this in the middle of Starbucks, I can't believe you."

Or, if you were listening to your motivational music and had to remove your earplugs...

"You made me miss the chorus to (insert song title here), I hope you're happy."

Once you've got this out of the way, the next goal is simply to get into a regular conversation.

THE CONVERSATION

You know what? Once you're over the very slight stumbling block that is the transition phase, the next goal is simply to get into an everyday normal conversation with the girl.

You don't really need to know a great many tips and tricks as the whole point of DDG is to keep the whole structure as simple as possible. Of course, I'll include a few strategies to help you out but the emphasis, at least in the early stages, should be to approach as many girls as possible so you can vanquish any approach anxiety you might have. Only after you've attenuated your AA, might you then want to think about incorporating some more advanced methods into your arsenal, just so you can have a few extra tools. You'll recall how it's my belief that overloading your head with these tools is a major cause of AA in the first place but once you're past it, learning how to properly kino escalate or how to make the most of your dates will be essential in order to move your relationships on to the next level. After all, if you're a bad first date, you ain't getting her into bed.

Moving on...

As a general rule, the longer you're engaged with a girl in conversation, the more solid a phone number is likely to be. Of course, there are exceptions, but generally, a girl will be more receptive to your follow up texts if your conversation lasted twenty minutes as opposed to only two. This is something you should exercise good judgement on. A two-minute conversation is often all that can be managed, if for example either of you are busy, in which case, you will have to make good with what you have. You also don't want the conversation to drag on for too long, otherwise you risk the girl assuming you have nothing else going on, which is hardly attractive. The absolute maximum I would deem necessary is twenty minutes, by which point you should have already made arrangements to meet her at some other time, and have taken her number. The only occasions I've gone over twenty minutes is when I've taken her on an instant date, which is something we'll discuss later.

Use this time to get to know the girl. What was she doing before you interrupted her? What area of town is she from? What does she do for study or work? How does she spend her free time?

I know how easy it is for our minds to go blank when we're in these situations, so you'll be pleased to know that in about 90% of instances, the girl will be happy to do the majority of the talking. Let her. Often, I struggle to get a word in myself, and it's never a problem.

No matter how much she rambles on, however, it's down to you, as the man, to take responsibility for directing the conversation to where it needs to go, which ultimately is discovering common ground so you can arrange a date and have a reason to take her number. Here are a couple of questions that will help achieve this:

- What are her interests?
- What does she like doing if she has a full day to herself?

If you both enjoy art galleries, for example, then that would be the logical place for your first date. Keep this in mind whilst conversing.

Although admittedly, these days, I don't ask these questions anymore, at least not for the purpose of arranging a date. Why? Because I'm getting older, I've been to every museum in town more times than I can count, and what if she was to say she likes marathons or ultra running. I'd be fucked.

No, these days I instead ask leading questions so we end up doing what I want to do but more importantly, it's where I know to be the best place to take a girl on a date - The bar. Which is why you can ask this simple question:

- What's your favourite bar around here?

If she doesn't drink, then just switch bar for coffee shop and aim to take your girl there.

Bar first, coffee shop second.

Simple.

Often, what happens is that you'll be in conversation with a girl and you'll realise that you're not actually that attracted to her. Maybe she's boring or not as hot close up as she was at a distance. When this happens, I tend to simply thank her for her time and move on. Nobody's lost anything and you still have a successful approach under your belt.

You might think I'm insane for doing this but there's an important lesson and psychological shift to learn here. By being the one to decline a girl, I'm putting myself in the position of selector. I mean, wasn't it me who made the approach in the first place? It's women who have one egg to the trillions of sperm, which is why society protects them at the expense of the other, and it's also why, at least in these post-patriarchal times, it's women who have all the power in the dating market, that it's they who are the gatekeepers of sex. Men hardly help themselves by fawning over women either, so when a rare man comes along and he's the one doing the picking and choosing, it's actually an incredibly rare find. She will realise this.

Approach women knowing that you're turning the tables, that you're the one who gets to decide. Go over to your next girl with an inquisitive mindset. Is she hot enough for you? Is she friendly and interesting enough for you? Will she make you laugh? Of course, this means that if it turns out she's not as great as you'd initially hoped, you must be willing to walk away.

Congratulations. You've just switched the entire dynamic and given yourself all the power.

GETTING HER PHONE NUMBER

Remember, it's actually quite important to have found common ground before you go for the phone number. You have to make it as logical as possible to meet up again because you both share a common interest. Of course, if none can be found, you always have bars and coffee shops to fall back on, and there's no harm in that.

Assuming you've just discovered you both like art galleries, art-house movies or Italian food, you can then just suggest that you should both go to the art gallery/movie theatre or the new Italian restaurant you heard is pretty good. You're not asking, you're suggesting. "We should go to the art gallery together." It's at this point you hand her your phone and tell her, "put your digits in here."

This is taking charge, showing you know what you're doing and demonstrating confidence, and we all know women want that in a guy.

Whilst she's tapping in her digits, a common mistake many guys make is to remain silent. A girl putting her magic digits into your phone is quite a heavy moment and I'm sure you might have noticed a change in the air when it happens. *Holy shit, she's actually doing it, I'd better keep quiet or she might change her mind.*

My advice is to keep the moment light by continuing to talk, if you can, maybe by remarking that the bar you have in mind is one of your favourites. If she has a friend with her, then you should definitely take those ten seconds to say a few words to her, "so how do you two know each other?" as doing this shows excellent people skills on your part and you never know, but when they're walking away, the friend might well comment about how friendly you were, which has to be better than risking being on the friend's wrong side for the sake of a little small talk.

Another common mistake, and I've done this more than once when I was starting out, is ending the interaction and then rushing off just as soon as you have her number. Getting the number is not the prize, you still have to get the girl on a date and just because you have the digits does not mean she'll answer your texts and then make the effort to dress up, come out and meet you. Please don't ruin things at this late stage just because you're feeling either nervous and wanting to get the hell out of there before saying something stupid, or euphoric and thinking only about the steak meal you're about to treat yourself with. You don't have to go overboard by remaining with her for another half an hour, in fact, a couple more minutes is more than enough, just don't be quick to run off thinking you have victory, is what I'm trying to emphasize.

But yes, once you have the number, it's then merely a matter of arranging the first date, which you'll do through text messages, finalizing the details you already broached during your interaction. My advice is not to play the three-day waiting game like a sixteen-year-old wondering what the fuck he's supposed to be doing. A few minutes earlier, you declared your interest, remember, so playing it cool now, all of a sudden, is to lack congruence and to come across as disingenuous. What I normally do is text immediately, as I'm walking away, though only briefly to say that now she has my number too and that I'll think about the exact time/location/details etc over the course of the day and fill her in when I know more. What this does is eliminate the sixteen-year-old boy shit immediately, she will usually always reply within a few minutes with something short like a thumbs-up emoji and then you're not on tenterhooks until you have the balls to finally text. Then all you need to do is decide when and where you're meeting and text her the details when you know what they are. Done.

There is, however, the option of taking the girl on a date immediately, which is a subject we'll cover next.

I've already written a full book on men's dating psychology; *First Date Mastery*, which elaborates in some detail how best to succeed on your date, explaining everything you need to know from start to finish. Whilst covering first dates is beyond the scope of this book, I shall briefly include the concept of instant dates because they're definitely something you should aim to take her on immediately following a direct pick up, whenever both your circumstances permit.

Instant dates (IDs) refer to meeting a girl and then going for coffee there and then, and you might be pleased to hear that they're surprisingly easy to carry out.

You have, after all, shown your worth and approached her cold and direct in the supermarket in the middle of the day. You've made your introductions and engaged in conversation for several minutes. You're attracted to her and because of your direct approach, you've shown confidence, balls, and I'm also willing to bet she's intrigued about learning more about you.

Why not push the envelope that little bit further?

Going for a coffee then and there is not only logical but sensible. So long as she's not busy then there's no reason why she shouldn't agree to your suggestion of, "do you have time to grab a coffee now?" It's for this reason that during your interaction, you need to ask what she was doing before you came bounding up the street, so that you can judge whether you should go for the instant date option, or instead wait until some other time yet to be determined. If she was in the middle of a shopping trip then there'll be no problem going to a bar or coffee shop with you right away. If she was heading for coffee anyway then ask to join her. If, as often happens, she's busy and in a rush, then don't worry, just can the idea of an ID and stick with the original plan of getting her number and texting to finalize the details as you normally would.

If the girl has time to spare then you can, and should, suggest coffee quickly. My record is about thirty seconds after meeting, though this is something you must learn to use your best judgement with. Obviously, the more receptive girls will be more willing to go for coffee relatively fast, because they'll be putty in your hands, and one of the best ways of judging how receptive they are is by how thrilled she looks, sounds and acts, as well as by her answer to the question, "what were you doing before I came along?" Most often, if they're not receptive, they'll say they were going to work and that they're in a rush, though obviously, this doesn't necessarily mean she doesn't like you, she might actually have one of those things called a job. If, however, she does have time to spare, then you may take this as a green light. When this happens, suggest going for a drink immediately.

When it comes to future flaking, there's a marked difference between speaking for a few minutes on the street and spending an hour in a bar or coffee shop. This is because by the end of the latter, she's already invested quite a bit of time into you and you're no longer just some random guy she met on the street. In fact, you're very likely to be the only guy in her entire life who she met and within ten minutes she was enjoying coffee with. You might even say, you literally swept her off her feet. How romantic. Women love this kind of thing and trust me, she'll tell all her friends about it.

Don't be surprised if the girl offers to pay. This happens frequently and you should allow it. By allowing the girl to invest her time, effort and now money into you, you're subtly making yourself even more enticing. We do, after all, value what we have to work for or invest in.

One of the most powerful things you can do during your ID (or any date) is to "qualify" the girl to your own standards. I've included the section on qualification from my book *First Date Mastery: The Complete First Date Psychology Guide For Men* in the bonus section below. Qualification is powerful. This is how you make her fall in love.

BONUS SECTION

- Qualification
- I Hope You're Friendly Too?
- Pre-Approach Priming

QUALIFICATION

I'm tempted to say that qualification is even more important than forging a connection with the girl, but for the simple reason that you won't get to qualification, or really even need it, if you build a good connection, I would still put the earlier section at the top of my list. But it's close.

Once again, I'll reiterate that building a strong connection is the most important thing you can do to make a girl want to see you again. But for now let's change that mindset because qualification is where YOU get to decide if you want to see HER again.

Qualification is something women are very, very good at. Indeed, because so many men throw themselves at women, they need to have a method of filtering out those men of lesser quality.

That method is qualification.

Women naturally qualify men because they grow up with an expectation of what their dream guy should be like. As they age and lose sexual market value, you'd think that women would eventually become more realistic and shorten their long fucking lists of qualifications but this is not what I have found. In fact, if anything, they become even more demanding at precisely the time they're running out of eggs and their chances of ever having a baby is reaching zero, and insanely, they maintain these ridiculous expectations of what they want in a man well into their senior years and beyond.

Did I ever say that women only date up?

And it's tough luck for any man who does not meet their unreasonable high expectations.

And if it wasn't hard before for men to qualify to the high expectations women have of men, now, in the age of Tinder, if anything, it's become even worse.

To put it mildly, girls have an incredibly long list to which men must comply in order for us to be worthy of their interest and investment. The following list is by no means exhaustive:

1. He must have a sense of humour.
2. He **MUST** be a doctor, lawyer or run his own successful business.
3. He must get me.
4. He must be caring and sensitive.
5. He must have an incredible body.

6. He must be handsome.
7. All my friends must also love him.
8. He must be confident.
9. He must be at least six feet tall.
10. He must drive an expensive car.
11. He must dress well.
12. He must have a big dick.
13. He must make at least six figures.
14. He must have a huge social circle, one that will potentially add value to me.
15. He must be well travelled and cultured.
16. He must have an education equal or preferably greater than mine.
17. He absolutely must, must, must earn more than me (this one is especially important).

This list will probably never end and the hotter the girl, the longer and more detailed the list will be and why not? She has men throwing themselves at her so why shouldn't she expect someone in the top 1% amongst his peers.

And such is the importance that men comply to the qualifications of women that they will often go out of their way to discover this information, and they'll be completely unapologetic in how they go about it.

Let's take a typical conversation on the average first date. In the below scenario, let's imagine the girl is studying to become a lawyer and therefore she has a realistic expectation that one day she'll be earning an above average salary:

Girl: So, what is it you do?

Guy: I'm doing an apprenticeship with Auto Mechanics in town / I work for the tax department / I'm an administrator / I work at Walmart.

Girl: Oh, so how long have you been doing that?

Guy: About 2 years.

Girl: But you also study as well, right? You're aiming for bigger and better things, I assume?

Guy: Ermm well, errmmm no.

When the guy senses her disappointment with what he does for a living and knowing he could lose her, he will now have to try extra hard to make up lost ground. But by this point, it's already too late. Once he has to try to get her to like him again, it's already game over in most situations and there are no tricks in some imaginary bag he can pull out to salvage the situation, perhaps short of showing her his trust fund or winning lottery ticket. The girl is hypergamous and she has decided that she is of higher status and therefore higher sexual market value than him.

What the girl did was qualify him to her expectations and he did not match up to what she wants in a man.

In days past, I might have attempted to salvage this unwinnable situation by thrusting out my chest, showing how proud I was to be doing (insert job here) and telling her how much of a difference I was making in the world, because there's honour in being a public servant, administrator or whatever. Back then I might have ploughed onwards, bided my time and played the same trick, attempting to qualify her to MY standards. These days I don't even bother, not because I don't believe these situations are completely unsalvageable - I know enough tricks to possibly turn some of them around - but because I recognise that even if I do win her back, it will only be temporary, and she will still arrive home after the date, have time to think things over and ultimately decide she's still of higher SMV than me, despite the incredible game I might have been able to play. These days, I tend to prefer an easier life and choose to stay away from the lawyer/doctor types, instead preferring to spend time with women where I'm not fighting a losing battle, at least until such time arrives when my zombie series makes me a millionaire.

We have learned that women qualify men with great ease but men doing the same to them has always been very hard for us. Unless you're in the top 1% of men, then generally women don't throw themselves at us and so we've not had to develop a method of dealing with filtering out the floods of women who're trying to inseminate themselves with our seed. Now, in this insane post-feminist era, it's harder than ever for us to use the same trick because women have been, and indeed still are, taking over our traditional gender roles, which is resulting in making men more expendable than ever before. Therefore, we are expected to take whatever we can get and be damned happy for the privilege.

No thanks.

Though conversely, all this means is that when some rare guy shows up and actually does qualify a girl to his standards, it can result in an even more profound effect than it might have done in previous years.

Remember the above list belonging to the typical woman? Below is what a typical guy's list looks like:

1. She must be hot.

Is it any wonder that women have such an advantage over us? Is it any wonder why it so often appears like it's they who get to do all the picking and choosing instead of men?

So, what would happen if we played them at their own game? What if we could qualify them to our own ridiculously high standards of what we need in a woman for us to even consider them?

Fortunately, this is very easy once you understand the principles and from then on we truly can play women at their own game and frustrate the hell out of them in the process.

I have observed that generally, the less attractive the girl, the easier she is to qualify. As women increase in sexual market value, in other words, the more physically attractive they are and the more options they have in the market, the more qualifications you'll need to apply. This should not come as a great surprise, though if you're on a date with a girl who dates lots of men then qualification will make you stand out far and above most dates she's ever had before.

The first thing you need to do is make a list, just like how she has. You don't have to actually write it down, although it might help, but you definitely need to have a very good idea of what it is you're looking for, what it is you really need in a girl.

Give the question some thought. What do you want in a girl?

Your list can, and should, include specific details about her looks, but this definitely works best if the list is broad and includes all kinds of other elements that together make up the larger part of it because its these things that will differentiate you from all the other guys who only care that she's hot.

What would your dream woman be like? Here's an example:

1. She must not be a single mother.
2. She must be solvent.
3. She must not have a worthless degree that I might end up paying for.
4. She must be ambitious.
5. She must not smoke.

6. She must not always merely follow the crowd but do her own thing.
7. She can hold a conversation.
8. She's clever.
9. She likes to travel and discover new places.
10. She can't be materialistic, I need a girl who can be happy without all those flashy things.
11. She has to be spontaneous. I need someone who can run out in the rain with me when it thunders and go crazy for no good reason.
12. She must be kind and generous.
13. She must be feminine.
14. She must not be a feminist.
15. She must love animals.
16. She must enjoy nature, going out into the wilderness and camping in the middle of nowhere.
17. She must workout a minimum of three times a week.
18. She must have her own hobbies and interests.
19. She must understand that I'm a busy man and must allow me peace and quiet to do my work.
20. She must be well read and enjoy reading.

You see what a list like this does?

It doesn't matter how attractive she is, if she doesn't tick the boxes on this list then she doesn't get a look in. You'll be the only guy she's ever known who would turn her down simply because she's not spontaneous.

Women are used to having all the power.

A list like this takes the power back.

And because of this, SHE has no choice but to chase YOU!

And she WILL chase you.

She'll chase you because you're different, you're the only guy she's ever met who's not drooling over her.

You're the only guy she's ever met who's used qualification.

So, now you have your list, how should you go about using it?

The best way to use this magical list is to be blunt, honest, open, deliberate and just ask her. Remember that the contents of this list are very important to you. So why not just ask her? She asked you about your job right? So play her at her own game.

Guy: You know, you're quite funny and I really like that and I can see that you know how to hold a conversation. But what I really want to know is ... *pauses for effect* are you the kind of girl who enjoys discovering new places? Do you like to travel and explore?

Remember that her answer is important to you, which is why you lean slightly back, fold your arms and look series.

No girl in the world is going to say "no" she doesn't like

discovering new places. The fact is it doesn't really matter. You're qualifying her based on something other than her looks and so far, she's passing your tests. Let her. The aim is to attempt to get her to impress you as much as possible because as humans, we attempt to impress people we like, ergo, if she's going to any length to answer your question, she can only deem subconsciously that it's because she likes you, even if she doesn't know it yet.

After this initial little bit of qualification, I would wait a bit before trying it again with a more important or profound point on your list. Since she's already talking about the places she's been and things she's discovered, you can use this opportunity to build upon the connection you already have, as spoken about earlier. What did she like so much about her trip to France/Italy/Japan?

When that conversation thread inevitably expends itself, you can then throw in another:

Guy: I really like spontaneous people. Would you say you're spontaneous?

Again, no girl in the world is going to say she's not spontaneous, even most men like to think of themselves as being spontaneous, at least to some extent because it is, after all, another word for *exciting,* is it not?

Let's go back to the conversation...

Girl: Oh, well, erm, yes I suppose I am spontaneous.

Guy: Awesome! Tell me one really spontaneous thing you've done in the last six months?

Now just sit back and wait for her reply.

Remember to make it look like it's important to you that she's spontaneous. It has to seem to her like it's possible that the answer she gives might disappoint you somehow, and this is an extremely important part of doing it right.

If she gives a typical girly answer, one that's not something which excites you then you need to act genuinely disappointed (breaking rapport as above).

Girl: Well, I was bored last week so I just phoned my friend and we decided to drive 50 miles to the next town for a shopping trip.

Guy: That's rubbish. Give me something else. Something really cool that's going to impress me.

Girl: OK, well, a few weeks ago I walked past a sign that said "join up for fencing lessons" and I thought, that's so cool, I've just got to give it a go, so I did.

It's important that if the spontaneous act she carried out is indeed impressive, then you need to let her know that you're impressed and that therefore she has your approval. You should then connect on what it is she said.

Equally important is that if it's a load of crap and you're not impressed one bit then you have to tell her how underwhelmed you are (in a half jokey, yet half serious way) and she's going to have to try harder to come up with something a little better.

I will point out again that what you're doing is getting HER to impress YOU.

Think about all the girls you've known throughout your life and how you've gone out of your way to impress the ones you like by boasting about your exploits or even showing off right in front of them. The act of attempting to impress the girl shows how she has you in her control and that she is of higher sexual market value than you. By phrasing your questions correctly and by being a little manipulative, you're turning the tables and instead prompting her to impress you.

She might very well start telling embellished tales of crazy exploits, like the time I was told by a girl she was a qualified pilot and I later found out she'd once had a flying lesson. When they start doing this, don't be turned off like how they almost certainly would be if you did the same thing but instead you should silently congratulate yourself because it means the date's going well.

The deeper the qualifying question, the more rapport or connection it's best to have before you ask it. For example, if you match on Tinder and immediately ask if she will allow you time to work without being constantly harassed and bothered, if she's a feminist or how often she lifts, then she's not very likely to care whether she conforms or not. Ditto for very early on during your first date. Use your best judgement with this very powerful technique.

An even easier, and sometimes more appropriate, method is to use qualifying *statements* instead of qualifying *questions*. These are less powerful because obviously, you're not prompting her to do any work to qualify to what you want in a girl but are instead making an observation and in effect telling her that she already complies to at least one of your qualifications. This is still subtly placing yourself above her.

Qualifying statements can be used so early on that often I will even use them as my opening line on Tinder. Say, for example, in one of her images she's cuddling a dog then you can begin by texting, "An animal lover ... I really like that! What are their names?" Likewise, if during the first few minutes of meeting she offers to buy the first round of drinks you could say, "awe, you're considerate ... I really like that," while giving her a rub on the back. By doing this you're still checking these attributes off your list, however you're not doing it by asking questions but by making statements and doing so in a way that she knows she's receiving your approval. Again, by doing this, you're subtly acting as the selector and therefore placing yourself above her in sexual market value, thus satisfying her hypergamy.

Once the date progresses and she's invested then you can slowly weave in as many qualifying questions as your best judgement deems you can get away with before you start coming across as being completely arrogant (remember to save some for the second date). However, even though it must be kept in mind that it's much better to come over as arrogant than somebody with no standards whatsoever, a smart man will use his judgement to find the right and most effective balance. Every girl is different, the hotter the girl, the more attention she's used to getting from other men, the more aggressive with qualification you might need to be. Unfortunately, as so often, this is one of those things you will improve at as you gain experience.

In conclusion, qualification is how you get women to try impressing you because what you're doing is subtly placing yourself as selector and therefore they need to demonstrate that they're on your level. I swear, this wouldn't work if women didn't have enormous egos and I have indeed found that qualification works best on some of the more egotistical women out there, certainly the more attractive women.

This is how the rich ugly guy gets the gorgeous girl because rich guys naturally use qualification all the time. They've already been there and done that, they've got the successful business and the car to prove it, and if a girl is even to get a look in with such a guy, then she has to prove she's worth his effort. Is she adventurous? Is she fun? Is she sporty? Is she kind? Is she intelligent? Is she good at conversation? - What's that? Yes, you say? Then prove it to me right now!

I HOPE YOU'RE FRIENDLY TOO?

Have you ever asked a girl if she's friendly?

If so, what did she say?

Did she say that no she wasn't friendly? I doubt it.

By working the question or statement "I hope you're friendly?" into your opening line you are, in fact, commanding her to be friendly.

"Hey, I was just stood over there with my friends and I saw you and thought, wow, she is stunning, so I literally just had to run over so I could say hi. I hope you're friendly too?"

You've already shown your worth by making this ballsy approach and now you're covertly telling her to show her worth back by being friendly.

No girl in the world is going to be a bitch after you've

paid her such a fine compliment, it's just not polite. You're also subtly communicating that you like friendly people. My suggestion is to phrase this statement more as a question that you tag on to the end of your direct opening line.

You can also use this technique again later on in your interaction by telling her, "hey, you know what I really like about you … I've only just met you but you're just so friendly."

I will explain the dynamic behind this by borrowing a section from my book *First Date Mastery, The Complete First Date Psychology Guide For Men.*

Start vvv

What I'm about to tell you is the most effective way of complimenting women. Not only will this technique work on a first date but it will also work exceptionally well in pick up situations, say, for example, if you were chatting to a girl in a bar or seeing her for the very first time in the coffee shop.

To explain this properly, I'll relate it to a scenario you may very well have experienced in your life.

When I was a young kid, nearly every day a group of us would play football in the local park. Anyone who's played football knows that the least enjoyable position to play is goalkeeper. Playing in goals involves standing around, having the ball struck at you full whack, diving on the badly maintained, cracked and rock solid grass and basically cutting your legs to shreds. However, my friends learned how to manipulate me into volunteering to play this position every time and to this day, I still have no idea if they knew what they were doing or if it was all accidental. They did it like this:

Friend:You're really good in nets, aren't you. You're fearless. I've never seen anyone so willing to stand in front of a football coming full speed at their face.

Me: Um, thanks.

Friend: Yeah, you can dive really far as well, and you have such great reactions. Have you ever thought about becoming a professional?

What my friends did was compliment me in an honest and sincere way but what appears to have been the most important detail is that they went into specifics as to WHY I was supposedly so good as a goalkeeper. For me, this meant that I did not want to disappoint them by altering this image they had of my goalkeeping skills.

Looking back, I recall putting in the extra practice on my own, trying to further improve my reactions or the distance I could dive. I even paid money to go on a goalkeeping course the local football club had organised, just so that this image they had of me would not be harmed.

Did your older brother ever once say, "I love you, you're so generous with your pocket money."

This is the exact technique older brothers have been using to fleece their younger siblings out of their money for centuries.

How can this technique be used to our advantage when it comes to the dating arena?

We already know that the only time in your life you should tell a girl she's hot is during a pick up situation, but what we can do is compliment her on something specific about how she looks, and when I say *looks*, I mean how she has chosen to *dress*, a small detail perhaps, or failing that, something about her personality.

When you're meeting a girl on a date, they will almost always wear something that makes them stand out; a scarf, bobble hat, the way they've done their hair, maybe a revealing tattoo, and the best time to mention this is immediately because it's odds on they've dressed this way especially for you. When you greet her, hold out your hand, take hers, kiss both cheeks, notice the thing that stands out and then say that you like whatever it is. Then give your very brief reason.

"That's a cool scarf ... matches your shoes. Right, are you ready to go in?"

"I like what you've done with your hair ... looks different to the photos. Right, are you ready to go in?"

After you've said it, move on, you're not fishing for any compliments for yourself here and neither do you really care if she appreciates the remark or not. In fact, you should not even frame it as a compliment at all but as an observation you've just made, and that therefore she has your approval. This way, instead of placing her above you in SMV, you're instead subtly placing yourself above her. Compare and contrast this way of doing things to the guy who shows up and immediately declares, "you're looking so beautiful today," before waiting to see how she reacts to what he thinks is a bold, daring and unique compliment.

Because compliments only really work if they're genuine, if you're complimenting something about her personality, make sure you've known her longer than five minutes first. If you tell her she's really intelligent before you've known her long enough to know whether this can even be true then it won't sound sincere and she might well wonder if you're trying to manipulate her or worse, that you're seeking her approval. Use your judgement.

If she's especially friendly then this is a particularly good compliment you can give. Once again, it needs to be elaborated upon slightly, in that it's best if you can give a quick reason as to why you think she's friendly. How I've done it to great effect is by saying something like, "you're really friendly, aren't you, you put people at ease and do most of the talking, which makes it easier for me ... just the way I like it," *sinks back into the seat with hands behind head*. Again, notice how I'm giving her my approval.

Can you see how this is so much better than mentioning her looks?

The added benefit of complimenting her friendliness is that unless you give her a good reason not to be friendly, she will now try her very best not to alter this image that you have of her in your head. She will not want to disappoint. If it's a compliment that she believes to be true, or would like to be true, then she'll do her best to make it appear true.

Can you see how the friendly compliment could also work in a pick up situation?

Girls are often very uneasy with pick ups and for good reason, they're just not practiced at being picked up. By telling a girl you met literally one minute earlier that she seems friendly, you're in fact commanding her to be friendly. This often works even if she's being closed and guarded and then you can watch in astonishment as her body opens out and she starts asking you questions while she becomes more talkative. All because you just told her she was friendly.

Again, there needs to be a specific reason for why you're making this compliment because to lack a reason is not to be genuine. You don't want her to see through it. Have a genuine reason as to why you think she's intelligent, friendly, caring or any other positive attribute and the compliment will be so much more powerful.

End ^^^

I wrote that with the first date or an ID in mind, but it can be used just as well during a pick up situation, as long as good judgement is exercised.

Give it a try and see how well it works.

PRE-APPROACH PRIMING

Whilst admittedly, pre-approach priming (PAP) is perhaps most effectively utilized at night, the daytime will present infinite opportunities to use this very easy, yet powerful tool to greatly improve your chances of engaging in a successful approach.

DDG involves approaching women cold, meaning you've had no prior contact with the person. What PAP does is warm up the prospect before your arrival, thus increasing your chances of the girl being receptive.

Studies have shown that toddlers bond much faster if they spend time waving and making hand signals from across the playpen. By instigating a "conversation" from across the room then by the time you make the introductions, there will already be some level of attachment. PAP can be as small as eye contact, a smile, eye contact with a smile or even a silently mouthed hello or a wave.

Very often, if women are attracted to you, they'll instigate this themselves. Generally, women do not approach men, that's not how things work unfortunately for us, but what they frequently like to do is give men little "come on" signals from across the room in the hope that he will initiate an approach. They do this because it's safe for them and requires very little confidence on their part.

Most men will have experienced some level of female papping throughout their lives, most likely in a night club or bar, though it can happen absolutely anywhere. The next time you're papped by a girl, my suggestion is to approach. Don't bother with the "I saw you from the other side of the room and thought you were stunning" routine, she's the one who spotted you, so instead go with something like, "you seem really friendly so I thought I'd come over to say hi."

Next time you're at the supermarket, try making eye contact with as many attractive women as you can. Watch for those who meet your eye with a smile. That's your invitation to approach. Don't hesitate, just go.

Again, because you've been "invited" to make an approach, my suggestion is to skip the opener as well as any fancy shit, and just go straight to the introduction, holding out your hand and saying, "I'm Terry," or whatever your name is. This works anywhere; the street, shopping mall or Starbucks.

At Starbucks, you might even take things a step further. Make eye contact, smile and wave. If she waves back then that's your invitation to approach. Just casually walk over, introduce yourself and take the chair beside her. Was approaching women ever so easy?

In a crowded and noisy bar, sometimes non-verbal communication is the only way to engage in an actual conversation. Try raising your glass in a gesture of cheers and see if it's returned.

You might assume PAP won't easily carry over to street pick ups because you're both in motion but you'd be wrong because the outdoors present plenty of opportunities. Making eye contact whilst passing a girl is beyond simple and sometimes, something as small as a simple nod can have the best results. Was the nod returned? Then consider your approach warmed. Park benches can make for extremely easy papping, though crosswalks are probably your best opportunity. I was once across the street from an attractive girl and the little green man was taking a long time to light. When we made eye contact, I tapped my wristwatch and pretended to yawn. She laughed. When the green man eventually appeared, I waited on my side for her to approach me and simply said, "hi, I'm Charlie."

At the gym, maybe wipe the sweat from your brow exaggeratedly or bench press thin air if this kind of comedy simulating is something consistent with your own personality.

The best thing is that PAP takes no balls at all and if your attempts are not reciprocated then you haven't lost anything, you haven't even made an approach.

Be creative with your PAPs, tailor them to your situation, ensure they're congruent to your own personality and have fun with them. If it appears you're just trying to amuse yourself and not overly dependent on the outcome then nothing bad can possibly come of it. She will be primed, ready and receptive for an approach.

Question: I've now had several attempts trying to get girls to stop but their eyes always seem to glaze over and they just carry on walking. What am I doing wrong?

The most likely reason is that you're not projecting yourself enough. Remember that you've seen something you really want so this must be reflected in your approach. Be passionate and dramatic. Project yourself! Be confident! Have belief that she'll stop for you! This can be common when starting out but like I said, apart from approach anxiety, getting the girl to stop is the hardest part of this game. At least you're making approaches so you're on your way. Maybe read the approaching sections again and always, always analyse every approach you do and think about how you might improve.

Don't forget, there are always shopping malls and coffee shops where the women are standing around or seated. That will be easier if stopping women is the problem. Girls sitting on benches are easiest of them all, so start there. If after all that you're still struggling then get feedback from a friend.

Question: Ok, I've given this a few tries and when girls are on their own I've had some success, but what do I do if the girl I like is with a friend?

Most often the girls you like will be with friends, that's just the way it is, so you should not allow this to stop you from approaching. One advantage of day game over night game is that there are different rules. During the day, her friend is more likely to be polite and should even be happy her friend is meeting someone.

Make sure you don't leave the friend out of the interaction so that she's standing there feeling awkward. Include her.

Sometimes I might tailor my initial approach if there's a friend, so that she's acknowledged, but it involves having to be pretty sharp with your observation. Notice something unique about the girl you like and then you can mention that as the outstanding feature that made you decide upon her over the friend. It would go something like this:

"Hey, I just saw you over there and had to come over to

say hi, because I think you're stunning." I would then glance at the friend and say, "I think you're attractive too, it's just that I've always had a thing for girls with…" it's at this point you would mention the outstanding feature. Failing that, you can play it safe by saying you've always had a thing for blondes/brunettes, assuming the two girls have different hair colours, otherwise you're screwed.

This is how you get on the good sides of both girls and there's no way the friend can be bitter or jealous after that little piece of charm, but you should also remember to involve her in the conversation going forward. Speak to the friend when your girl is occupied putting her number in your phone, for example, "so how do you two know each other?"

Question: What if there are two friends?

No difference in principle, though eventually it becomes like juggling or plate spinning. Congratulations if you have the guts to do this, especially when there are far easier targets to go for.

Question: What if the room's really crowded with people and I'm worried about embarrassing her?

Well, first of all, the overwhelming vast majority of women absolutely love being the centre of attention. Attention is like crack cocaine to most women so there's no reason to be concerned about embarrassing her.

Are you sure this isn't about you? Because second of all, let's take a crowded subway carriage and make the incorrect assumption that everybody cares about your business and that ninety people are all listening in to your conversation. Now answer this. The next day when you're still regretting not approaching that girl because of all those eavesdroppers, will you still remember any of these other people? Are you still going to care about them when you're still thinking about the girl you let go?

Admittedly, I've had a few instances where I've delayed my approach until the right moment. If, for example, the girl I'm interested in as at the front of the queue at the coffee shop or having what looks like an important meeting, then if I was to approach at that moment, I'd only come across as socially uncalibrated and from then on, it would be too much of an uphill battle to salvage. You can make good with this, though, and should even acknowledge your earlier cowardice when you finally come to speak with her. This is extra important in case she saw you inside the shop, and trust me, women notice everything. What I've done is follow her out of the coffee shop, done my usual opener and then added, "I saw you inside Starbucks but I just didn't have the guts to approach you then." This is funny because obviously, I do have the balls to approach and if you say it right, it never fails to get a laugh and then you're in.

Question: What if the girl I really like is

talking on her phone? This happens way too often.

You're right and it's a constant irritation of mine too. Phones, phones, phones. When I started out, I actually took a DDG class that involved walking around London with a private instructor looking for girls. It wasn't cheap, but anyway. I was told to always approach regardless of the girl being on her phone. You're a man, right, so her speaking to her mum, friend or boss shouldn't make a difference. However, after trying it several times, as well as witnessing my instructor making several unsuccessful attempts, I came to the conclusion that it's often too difficult an approach to make.

Why doesn't it work? For the simple reason that it's rude and you'll only trigger her ire. Even the sweet girls will be pissed off at having some guy talking to her whilst she's got a phone plugged to her ear, it's too much to concentrate on. Put yourself in her shoes, you know I'm right. I'm sure the world's best pick up artists might have no problem with this, but I'm trying to teach the average guy here, normal people, and my advice is to keep things as simple as possible. Why make DDG any more difficult for yourself when there's a cute girl sitting in Starbucks reading a book or a cheerleader with a broken leg hobbling on crutches.

In the past, I've been known to wait around for a girl to finish her call before making a move but only if she was particularly to my tastes. Other than that, though, there's not much else you can do. I've also been known to get tired of waiting and left it. Who wants to date a girl who's always on the phone anyway?

However, girls texting or otherwise dithering on the phone, which is most of the time these days, are highly receptive to approaches, so I would treat this situation more favourably.

Question: The only time I get out of the office to do some DDG is at lunch when all the girls are eating. I hate the thought of approaching girls when they're eating.

Yes me too. I think it bothers us guys more than it bothers the women though. Similar to the cell phone, wait for her to finish or find something easier. Always use your common sense in these situations.

Question: I stopped this girl in the street and she has a boyfriend, but I really like her. Any extra tips you can give?

Put yourself in the position of the boyfriend. How will you feel if somebody reading this book approaches your girlfriend when you're at work? You'd want your girlfriend to do the right thing and be truthful, wouldn't you?

This will happen often and when it does, I tend to just thank her for her time and say how lucky the guy is to be dating the kind of girl who wouldn't cheat on him. I've been known to add them on Facebook, because hey, you never know, they might break up a few weeks or months down the line. That's why it pays to be respectful because she might recall your approach and contact you at some point in the future.

Question: Damn iPhones, I stopped this girl and she's adding me on Facebook but my profile's a mess. This is really going to ruin my chances. What can I do?

Oh, man, social media. I wrote a book on Facebook game but it's so out of date that I would not suggest even looking at it. Social media changes every other month, so it was always going to happen.

If you add each other, she'll no doubt scrutinise your profile with a fine-toothed comb and I'm willing to bet you'll do the same. I've had women go back to the very start of my timeline to dig up information about me, right down to the murky depths of my past where all the breakdancing videos and old jobs and friends are kept.

It might be best to stay off social media entirely but I do recognise that it can be used to your advantage if done right. Just make sure you paint yourself in as positive a light as possible, which means not posting every hour with every little update to your life. No meal photos and images of drunken nights out. More than anything else, women hate seeing men posing topless in front of the mirror and for whatever reason, this is all men put up on

Tinder and other dating profiles. Guy's, please stop this! Selfies are not great either. Delete posts that make your life appear boring or mundane and make sure it doesn't look like you spend your life on Facebook, Instagram or whatever it is.

That doesn't leave you with much, does it, which is exactly the point. Intrigue will never count against you, just so you know.

So what should you include? My Facebook profile picture is of me at a Tough Mudder event. I'm covered in mud and happened to be photographed by a professional with one hand grabbing onto a swinging bar, a half-second before being flung through the air. It shows that I'm fun, sporty and up for life. Other than that, the only photos I have are when I'm out with friends, engaging in sports, travelling or with my mum's dogs.

Question: What about kino escalation?

Kino escalation is always a good idea and I recommend beginning right from your introduction with a handshake. From there you should try getting in little touches whenever possible but only when it makes sense to do so. It's easy to give a tap on the girl's elbow when you're emphasising a point, and I always recommend kissing the girl on both cheeks when you say your goodbyes.

Question: Should I try peacocking?

Erm, not really. I would just dress as yourself and don't

try to be anything you're not. Wearing silly hats to stand out is just a little weird for me.

I did discover a nice little tip quite by accident when I was working in Manchester. A florist was handing out free plants in tiny pots about the size of nectarines along with a business card to promote her business. I managed to snag three of these little plants. After work, I then had a long walk back to my car and I was amazed by the number of glances I was getting from women whilst I was carrying these three tiny and exceptionally cute plants. The next day, I went to the shop and made a few purchases of the same with the intention of doing some approaches. Let's just say, it went well.

Seriously, if you want to "peacock" or even get some super easy PAPs, buy some tiny plant pots, germinate some seeds and when they sprout, take them for a walk. Daisies work very well ;) Carrying one doesn't have the same effect as walking around with several, so get yourself a tray and fill it up so that maybe it looks like you're transforming your new flat, or something. You'll draw attention, for sure. Ask if she'd like to babysit one of your plants but make her promise to return it on your date. This similar to what Neil Strauss does in his book The Game when he mentions giving girls bracelets, trinkets or necklaces they have to return when they next meet. A plant's even better because she has to be responsible for it.

Question: Is going direct really the best

method for day game? I've read other PUAs recommend only going indirect.

Many PUAs will prefer indirect to direct, even in the day time, and if that's all they practice then they'll excel at that style over mine. I excel at DDG because it's the only method I ever use and I hope that throughout the course of this book, I've made a strong case for it. I will say that these days, more and more people are coming around to what I advocate for here because the results speak for themselves.

Question: I read that if you walk up to a girl and tell her she's stunning, you're giving away all your power because she knows she already has you without having to do anything. Charlie, what do you have to say about this?

There will be some women who will be put off by the direct approach, though to be honest, I haven't met many at all. The advantages of DDG far outweigh any disadvantages such as giving away any power to the girl you've just told is stunning. But it's a fair point and over the years, I've given it much thought, which is why I often add into my openers, "I really hope you're friendly too." By doing this, you're anticipating that particular potential problem and, hopefully, mitigating it, taking the power back, and demonstrating that while yes she might be stunning, but that you still haven't made your mind up about her. By dropping those few extra words into the opener, you're demonstrating that her looks aren't absolutely everything and that she must also prove she has something else to offer.

I will also point out that once I've called a girl hot or stunning in the opener, she will very rarely ever hear me use that compliment again (please see above bonus section for my explanation).

Question: So you've been doing this a while, huh? You must have some pretty funny stories?

I once approached a girl I'd worked with a couple of years earlier, I just didn't recognise her. When that happens, you've just got to laugh about it and grind on. Six months later, I was working with her again on another job, which might have been embarrassing except my girlfriend at the time was also working on the job, and my girlfriend was hotter.

My former instructor had lots of funny stories. He went day gaming so often that he approached the same girl twice within the same month using the same line, and that was in London, a city of 8 million people. His approach was indirect and I don't think it had the same effect, at least, definitely not the second time. Apparently, he just persisted as though he'd never seen her before. I wish I knew what was going through her mind ... ugh, men, haha.

When you start making lots of approaches, the unexpected will often happen and it's those occurrences you'll look back on with fondness. Before long, you'll also have funny stories of your own. The key is not to let the unexpected affect you. Confident guys do not let things out of their control dictate their feelings, emotions or state. When you start doing plenty of approaches, you'll find you remember the good ones and forget the bad. Your life will also improve because you'll make all kinds of new friends.

Question: I'm suffering from extreme approach anxiety. Sometimes I walk around for hours and I pass up so many opportunities to speak to girls, I just always cop-out. What can I do?

Hey, I feel for you, I've been there, in fact, I probably had approach anxiety even worse than you did. I'm assuming you've been learning so much material that it's making your head spin, right?

As I said earlier, I had more guts approaching girls *before* I started learning about pick up. AA is frequently exacerbated by filling your head with all these techniques trying to become the perfect pick up artist before you've even made a single approach. It's an impossible feat to achieve.

As I state in my other book *Destroy Approach Anxiety*, the key is to forget everything you know and go back to basics. Those basics are what you've learned in this book. Keep it simple.

If you really want to meet someone special then make a commitment to yourself. Invest in this. Do what I did, go to a strange city, hire an instructor, pay your money, book a nice hotel and make a promise that if you can approach twenty girls over the course of one or two days then you'll treat yourself to the greatest steak dinner you've ever had in your life. How good will that taste?

Question: Most of the best women are at the gym, yet you only briefly mention this as a place for pick up, and only then to use the indirect method. Can you elaborate?

Yes. A few years back, I ran a website on the subject of day game and one of the most popular searches that people would use to find my site was by using the search terms "pick up women at the gym" or "gym pick up."

Through having tried direct game at the gym several times and not having experienced the same success, it has become my belief that DDG is probably not the best approach for that environment.

Gym game requires its own category. Gyms in many ways more closely resemble bars and night clubs than supermarkets or coffee shops. At the gym, people, women especially, wear alluring attire and put on a front whilst exercising, just as they do in night clubs.

A typical direct opener at best loses its power, or at worst, it can come across as being creepy and yes, I've tested this, too many times, in fact, and so I've now come to the conclusion that perhaps the best method for gym pick up is a more indirect one, perhaps even the long indirect game. Though my advice is to treat your gym, that place where you exercise every single day, the same as you might your college course or existing social circle, in that you probably shouldn't shit where you eat. If, however, there's a girl you just can't get over then my advice is to work on yourself, become an attractive prospect that can't be resisted and make her come to you. Of course, all men should be doing this anyway.

Question: What other PAP signals have you got under your belt?

There's an endless amount of possibilities, which depend on your location and situation, though the best ones are always spontaneous.

If you're in Starbucks or the library and catch her eye over the top of your book, maybe you could yawn or pretend to fall asleep. Maybe point to her, yourself, back to her and then make the gesture for drinking coffee ... hint, hint.

At the gym, you can flex a muscle or bench press thin air. There's always the universal sticking out of tongue that can be used anywhere and waves are understood in any country. Remember never to underestimate eye contact with a simple smile from across the room. Often, that's all you'll ever need.

Well that's it. I've made it as simple as I possibly can because it really should be simple.

So now I want you to promise me one thing. Do not buy any more pick up books, read any more forum posts or watch any more Youtube approach videos until you've made at least ten approaches yourself.

You really do need to complete level one in the field before you try to skip to level ten in your head.

I understand that many guys reading this will be nervous as hell about approaching beautiful women in the street and telling them how stunning they are. Believe me, it really does get easier and if you can do this then you can do anything, you will feel it in yourself, and it will improve your life in ways you can't imagine.

The next time you see a girl you're attracted to, do not

allow her to simply walk out of your life. You owe it to yourself to see what might be.

You now know all you need to know to make this happen. All you need now is belief in yourself.

If you've enjoyed this book and feel that others might benefit from the content then please leave an honest review on the page you made the purchase. Don't forget to check out my other books also.

I'm wishing you all the luck in the world.

Charlie Valentino.

First Date Mastery

Confidence For Men

Online Dating For Men

Destroy Approach Anxiety